MW01674915

MANTRI PRAGADA MARKANDEYULU
[B Com, DBM, PGDCA, DCCP]
Novelist, Poet, Song &
Storywriter, Songwriter
Hyderabad - Telangana State – India
Email: mrkndyl@gmail.com

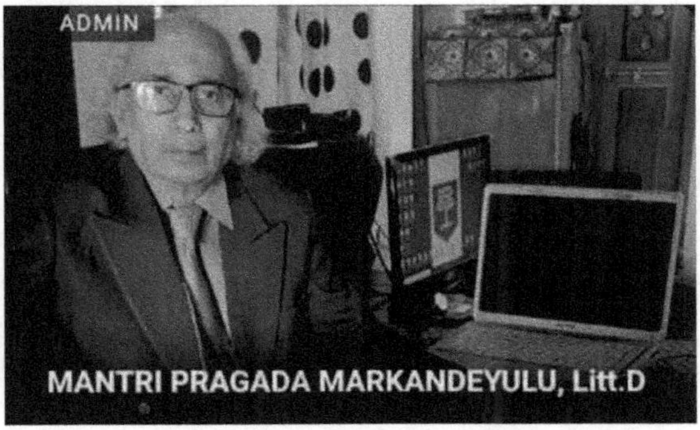

TALES OF YESTER-YEARS

Index:

A Real Story of a Russian

(People with weak mind Please don't read)

BACK FROM THE DEAD

(ENJOYED HIS LAVISH BIRTHDAY PARTY AND DIED)

Quote –

"Death is a depressingly inevitable consequence of life, but now scientists believe they may have found some light at the end of the tunnel.

The largest ever medical study into near-death and out-of-body experiences has discovered that some awareness may continue even after the brain has shut down completely."

–Unquote

BACK FROM THE DEAD:

Some times and on some occasions and at some Countries/places, it happens really in few cases, that dead persons come alive and participate in functions.

Quote-
"A Russian who was declared dead from drinking too much Vodka, returned from the dead to join in on the party being conducted in his memory.
His friends panicked and called the Police after he "partied too hard".
He was taken in an ambulance to the nearest hospital but declared dead on arrival.
The guards at the morgue were shocked when he had a "miraculous awakening" and then returned to continue partying, this time in the celebration of his rebirth"
– Unquote

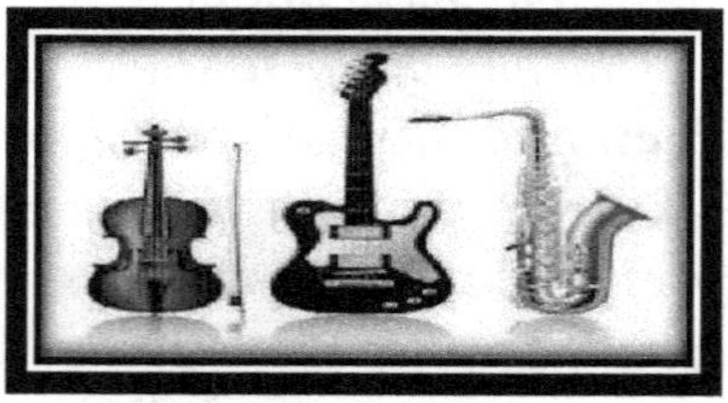

PARTY TIME

O My Friends, I Never Drank
No, no, I Never Drank
I Only Had a Small Pint
To warm up the Body and Mind ||

You Drink, You Drink
Enjoy and Enjoy the Cocktail Enjoy

A Day Rolled, Never Come Back
This Day, an Entertainment Day ||

I Know, Everybody Likes Vodka
They Give Jerk, That They Never Take
But Feels Like to Have Wine
Time Rolls Away, Take and Take the Drink ||

Have a Pint and Tell the Truth
The Cocktail Gives You Power and Kick
I Know, Your Tongue Will Like Vodka
Come on and come on, Have the Sip ||

Drink and Dance the Way You Like
This Party Is a Cocktail One
Have the Drink and Show the Way
Try to Shake the Body and Legs ||

Dance to the Music of Melody
Never seen before the Dancing Beauties
Dance and Step with Lanky Legs
Time is Rolling in a Dancing Way ||

Beauty like Queens are hosting one
Dance and Dance to the Sound of Music
Blow the Mind with Blowing Sound
Music and Dance is a Party Feature ||

Shake the Leg with your Vibrant Body

Music World is a Dance of Gift
Shine and Shine with Dancing Legends
Music and Dance is a Nature's Combo ||

Music makes the World so high
Music brings the Angels to Dance
Angels like the Music and Dance
The Earth, a place for Dancing Styles ||

Drink and dine, a system in life
Sing and Dance, a routine in style
Dance like an Angle, make the Soul feel happy
Life to move like an Angel's way ||

Full details of this incident are as follows; this incident took place in Russia:

One Russian celebrated his birthday function at one Star Hotel.
All friends were invited.

In that party, all types of drinks including vodka, whisky, gin, brandy, rum etc. were served and all the friends were asked to enjoy from morning to night.
No time limit was set.

The Russian and his friends booked Hotel Rooms, and right from morning to midnight, drink, eat, dance, enjoy music etc. all times, as per one's wish.

All the friends used to drink what they want up to deep neck.

ON FIRST DAY

This Russian had too much of drink and suddenly died during the course of drink party.
The Doctor from nearby Hotel called for, for medical check-up and treatment to this Russian.

Everybody felt sad about this incident, which took place on the very first day.
One Doctor, after medical check-up, declared that this person is dead.

Few of family members took this Russian to the nearest hospital.
But the party was going on in full swing.

Most of the partying friends were unaware of this incident because they were in their own world with too much of drinks and high state of condition.

At the Hospital also, the Doctors after verifying the complete body check-up came to conclusion that this man was brought 'dead'.

With the request of this dead man's relatives, the 'dead body' was kept in the mortuary of the hospital.

The news spread to his friends at the Hotel where the party was going on.
Some of friends got disturbed and some friends were not able to understand what happened to the hosting friend.

Some friends were very high on alcohol consumption.

The Russian family members decided that the party at the Hotel to continue, as per original schedule i.e., for one complete week.

This was in memory of the departed Russian, as Soul to rest in peace, the party since continued.

All friends were in one way felt very happy about this decision.
Every guest was happy.

All others are too good in sober condition.
There was no control for drinks.

Totally all the invitees/friends were drinking, dining, eating, dancing, all things are going on at the partying hotel.

All people took self-decisions to enjoy the entire week.
Because, everything was free.
No need to pay any money to anybody.
The entire hotel bill including that of rooms were at the cost of the hosting Russian family. Each invitee was a millionaire.
Each friend was moneyed person.
Everybody was a big business shot.
Each day, drink, drink and drink.
Nobody asks them or nobody to question them.
As a mark of respect, all the friends maintained two minutes silence as a mark of respect to the departed Soul.
All people again confirmed to continue this party, as usual.
All people are in full condition.
Few people are eating.
Few people are dancing.
There was also a cabaret dance on the stage, which was organized by the Hotel Management.
Most of the friends were smoking too.
Few people were playing cards.
All were enjoying as per their own wish.

NEXT DAY MORNING

The Russian whose dead body at mortuary, woke-up in the presence of mortuary staff and guards, stood-up and came back to the Hotel where the party was going on.

The Hospital security guards and staff became aghast, 'as the dead man from the mortuary became alive'.

This news became viral in the hospital.
All the relatives of this Russian were surprised.
Some relatives even feared for this incident.

They thought that how a dead man become alive and attend the party which he was hosting to his friends.

Even the Russian friends were afraid of his coming back to the hotel.

The party at the Hotel continued for the entire week.

In this party, the Russian who died and returned back to hotel for partying with friends, enjoyed a lot and lot with all types of drinks, eating, dining, dancing and there was not control of people during the party.

On the last day of the party at Hotel, this Russian was in high state of in-abbreviated condition and at midnight 1200 hours, he fell down and died, as everybody witnessed this incident.

This information and incident were informed to Police and in Ambulance, the dead Russian was taken to the same hospital, where he was taken earlier a week ago.

Hospital Doctors, Nurses and other staff feared for this, as once this Russian was declared dead and again, he was brought in Ambulance after becoming second time dead.

After testing and verifying the 'Russian Body', he was declared as' brought dead' and was accordingly issued with "Death Certificate".

This Russian dead body was handed over to his relatives.
The dead body taken direct to his home.
At Hotel, friends were in too much in-abbreviated condition.

Friends' brain was not working.
They were in high condition.

After the party was over, friends could know that the host “Russian was really dead. People and friends felt sorry for this.

But condolence meetings were conducted and prayed for the dead man’s Soul be rest in peace.

………

FASCINATING ALCHEMISTS
Aghoris Action with an American Journalist

AGHORIS:

Who are Aghoris?

What do they actually do and why do they only come out in public during Kumbhs?

"Aghor", "Aughad", "Kapalik", "Aghori", "Aughar", "Awadhoot" means the same, which is simple and natural state of consciousness.

The Aghora is a very vast subject, but here it is being explained in brief, a very little bit, as the readers may be able to know about the Aghori and their acts who are engaged in post-mortem rituals on dead bodies.

Mainstream Dharma (Sanathana Dharma) believes that ultimate goal of life is to attain salvation, but it is not at the cost of worldly pleasures.

This is according to Vedas - Brahmacharya, Grihastha, Vanaprastha, Sannyasa are mandatory in mainstream dharma and one should not willingly skip any of the above and Sanathana Dharma emphasize on individual contribution to society.

Aghoris the most fascinating alchemists:

Aghoris are the most advanced tantriks.

They have mastered the tantra sastra which is also a branch of Yoga.

The entire space which we call as Aakash seems to be an empty, but in reality, it is filled with full of unseen energies.

This Aakash is filled with energies which are nothing but, positively, negatively and neutrally charged atoms and molecules of elements.

In science, these are called electrons protons and neutrons.

These are also called as elecrolytes which mean carrying positive, negative and neutral energies or polarities.

All the physical forms are the essential building blocks of this basic form of these three energies.

Aghoris are the most powerful alchemists and they can associate various atoms from the space and form a physical structure and they can also change the physical structure into any other different physical form. In short, they are the best molecule manipulators.

When the structures are changed, their functions are changed automatically.

The Aghoris always live a secondary life, mostly in the jungles or in the grave-yards.

They can be compared to the scientists who also invent different elements by the manipulation of atomic structure or a particular substance.

There is a very fascinating story about these Aghoris narrated by the famous Paul Brunton, an American Journalist, who was specially sponsored by some of the rich people and sent to India to find out various genuine saints, yogis having yogic armistice powers.

He also lent about these Aghoris and he arrived at one place in order to have an interview with one Aghori who was supposed to stay at a remote place at the outskirts of a certain village.

There he enlisted a local person who initially was reluctant to follow Paul Brunton to meet the so called Aghori and interview him.

Because, the local guy was very much scared of this Aghori.

A lot of roomers was spread about the Aghoris.

Finally, Paul Brunton arrived at the spot where the Aghori was staying alone.

When the Aghori noticed these two people approaching him, he tried to scare them by throwing stones.

The local guy was very much scared, but the Paul Brunton pursued him that the Aghori was trying to scare us, as the stones were directed at a wrong place, as the Aghori only wanted to scare them and dissuade them not to approach him.

But Paul Brunton courageously approached this Aghori, and all of a sudden, the Aghori had become calm and quiet and with a lot of courtesy invited Paul Brunton and offered him a seat on a stone.

Then he turned to the local guy and addressed him in the local language stating that the Paul Brunton was his guest and in order to honour his guest, he ordered this local guy to cut a small piece from the dead body which was lying on a bank of a small lake near his ashram.

The local guy was dam scared, but he was more scared about the Aghori than the dead body. Aghori gave him a small knife and the local guy gathering his bits slowly approached the dead body reluctantly with closed eyes, he cut a small piece of flush from this dead body.

Paul Brunton was very much surprised by watching this drama as a spectator.

Finally, the local guy came back and handed over the small piece of flush which he took out from the dead body.

Then this Aghori noticed that this local guy cut his finger while attempting to cut the flush from the dead body.

The blood was running down, and this Aghori placed his hands on the bleeding finger, and said Oh My God, you are bleeding.

Don't worry. Now your small wound is healing.

When the Aghori removed his hand, there was no trace of any blood or that small cut which was also noticed by Paul Brunton.

Again, the Aghori went inside, he took out a clay pot, poured some water placed his vet, the flush from the dead body and he started cooking on the fire.

Without any word Paul Brunton was watching the drama as he was very much astonished.

After a while, the Aghori brought some leaves of a nearby tree, washed them with water and he placed couple of Ron structures which were looking like small balls on these leaves.

One leaf he offered to local guy and the other one to the Paul Brunton and to his shock the local guy noticed it was nothing but Rasgulla. It was not dead flush.

It was not the flush from the dead body.

The local guy explained to Paul Brunton, it was called Rasgulla, which was a sweet meat. Then the Aghori politely offered these Rasgullas to Paul Brunton.

When tasted by Paul Brunton it was so sweet and a lot of juicy syrup was oozing out and both of them enjoyed.

This is how that Aghori who mastered the tantra sastra, the science of tantra changed the molecular structure of this flush from the dead body and transformed to Rasgulla by changing the molecular structure.

This is what is called as a manipulation of the atom of molecular structure.

You disassociate a particular physical structure and re-arrange the atoms of the molecules from the same physical structure to rebuild another physical structure when the structure changes the function will also change.

That is why, we call the Aghoris are the most powerful and affective alchemists.

But they are misunderstood by lot of people, because no person will be daring enough to approach them and study them from close quarters.

Roomers always spread in a negative way and the people will go on adding their own whims and fancies and often depict Aghoris as bad guys.

The knowledge is very powerful, for that matter any knowledge, and even what the modern scientists are doing now-a-days.

When Alfred Noble Discovered Dynamite, the same dynamite was used in breaking the rocky structures to build the houses.

The same dynamite is also used by the terrorists to destroy the human beings.

The same way, same is the case with Aghoris. By mastering the tantra sastra and by practicing certain rituals they have evolved themselves to higher dimensions where they are capable of manipulating the energies of the five elements, the Earth, the Water, the Fire, the Wind and the Space.

By manipulating the atomic structures of these five elements, Aghoris can easily change the physical structures into different physical structures carrying out different functions.

They can change a solid particle to the liquid particle like from the element Earth to the element Water, same they can change into element Fire, and the element of Fire to other two elements.

This was the experience of Paul Brunton had when he encountered this particular Agohri. For them, the dead body, it is the combination of five elements.

Hence, they do not fear the dead bodies or the death.

That is why they roam around the jungles and grave yard, where human beings do not visit.

In our Puranas Maharshi Durvasa created kurtchya, the most dangerous and negative entity to kill Ambarisha who was rescued, protected and rescued by Lord Maha Vishnu and Sage Durvasa had to ask for a forgiveness for Ambarisha.

We dismiss as this a myth, but Late Shri Narayanadutta Srimali had wrote a book who himself was a great tantric. In this book he narrated an incident where a most powerful Aghori created this krutchya in order to create and havoc among the other Aghories and Yogis who assembled for a meeting.

Then the most respected and tantric guru Sri Nitynanada Swamy who was a benevolent sage, destroyed this krutchya with his powers.

These are the powers of Aghoris, some are used for benevolent purpose and some others use to scare people and become a leader.

AGHORA RISHI

In Shree Rudham from Yajurvedam, you shall come across "Aghora Rishi" could be another name of Lord Shiva.

Aghori or Aghora are people whose principles derived from Advaita of Sanathana Dharma performs spiritual practices to get salvation.

The Aghori (Sanskrit aghora) are ascetic Shaiva sadhus.

The Aghori are known to engage in post-mortem rituals.

Aghora may refer to The Hindu God Bhairava, a form of Shiva.

Aghoris feel that the sadhana in cremation ground removes fear.

Ø to get rid of sexual desires, Aghoris, sometimes, does sexual practice on the dead bodies.
Ø to avoid shame, Aghoris, all the time stay naked

Most of the people are afraid and scared of Aghoris, because of their powers and Aghori have number of names in the country.

The Aghori is also known as Kapalika and Kalamukhas.

The Aghori goes on practicing this soul of the Aghori is set free and it obtains moksha.

The culture of Aghori was started by a person Baba Kina Ram.

He was said to have lived for 150 years.

He died in the 18th century as his followers continued to spread his teachings.

Some fear that Aghori knows little about their practices and Aghori practices mostly on children, which people are afraid of them.

For this reason, Aghori are considered responsible for crime or the other.

Some people also feel and have apprehensions that Aghori kills innocent people.
It is not Fiction, but it is a Fact:

However, this may not be true as Aghori perform sadhana on dead bodies but they do not kill people for their needs.

Some people believe that Aghori has super powers and they want to make the most of these powers and get benefited.

Some Hindus say that it is true that Aghori can help with a lot of problems but if we seek help from an Aghori to solve a problem it may give rise to many more problems.

The Aghori never bother about what society feels about them and they live secret lives without any intention to get social recognition

Aghoris Holy Book is called Avadhuta Gita.

This Avadhuta Gita Holy Book contains a sacred text or all their teachings and beliefs.

The book specifies that Baba Keena Ram was the founder and the Adiguru of Aghori tradition.

The book also justifies that Lord Shiva spent most of his time in cremation ground doing sadhana.

Aghori Accessories:

Some say that Baba Keena Ram was the incarnation of Lord Shiva himself.

The Hindus do believe that Lord Dattatreya was the incarnation of Lord Vishnu, Brahma and Shiva all in single body.

The Aghori goes into complete darkness and lives till they get self-realization and they use corpses to invoke the mother Goddess known as Shamshan Tara.

They consider Shamshan Taraas one of the ten wisdom Goddesses and She has the power to Bless the Aghori with supernatural powers.

The mahavidyas that the Aghori religiously worship is Bhairavi, Bagalamukhi and Dhumavati.

The male God which the Aghori worships is Lord Shiva in the form of Bhairava, Mahakala and Virabhadra.

Let us try to find out from a neutral perspective about the truths behind these and how the Aghoris themselves perceive this.

1. An Aghori performs all seemingly nasty acts because it is a way to realize that nothing is impure or unclean.

2. If one can see purity in everything that is the highest state of Divine Bliss

3. At the core of these seemingly raw and savage sadhus is a highly realized soul who is above all dualities of nature.

Please note that this only holds good for genuine Aghori Sadhus and not anyone pretending to be one.

VISION AND REMEDIES ON DIVORCE

Marriages and performing marriages are very old traditions. Marriages are performed in great style. During the marriage functions, huge amounts are spent, for various purposes. Marriage is a onetime function in one's life. Everybody hopes and expects that the bride and bridegroom should lead a happy marriage life. After marriage, both bride and bridegroom should understand each other in every aspect, including financial, domestic, relationships and also professional career aspects. It is, of course, to have a good insight on these aspects. In earlier years, say during 1950's to 2000's, many marriages that took place and were successfully established their family in spite of many difficulties including financial aspects. The problems were not there with the husband and wife till 2000 year.

The problems slowly started emanating since the introduction of computerization. Everybody became qualified, everybody became software engineers and everybody became earning members. Moreover, huge salaries were being received especially by the ITeans in the IT sector. Slowly, likes and dislikes started amongst many newly-wed couple. One does not know why? There was lot of resentments with the newly married people. The reasons are self-explanatory and may be plenty. During the recent past, mostly in IT field who were working on software side and other related fields, love affairs became common. Many marriages took place. Simultaneously, there were many divorce cases. The reasons for divorce are not well known. Some people work at America, some people work at UK, some at Singapore, Australia, and Germany etc.

Generally, software people, who ones leave India for careers sake, never return to India. People get settled at somewhere in some country. They even become green card holders. These people never bothered to get married up to the age of 35-40 years. Many of the divorce cases are pending in various courts in India. These cases go on dragging. Even parents are never bothered about their children's marriage performance.

One B Tech Itean marriage took place in India four years back with one B Tech girl. Both went to America. What transpired between them was not known. The girl opted for divorce. The divorce came after 5 years. The bridegroom had paid compensation around Rs 10.00 lakhs to the bride. There were several divorce cases pending in the courts for want of divorce. It looks that divorce has become common and regular feature. On many petty, silly and waste matters, young couples are opting for divorce. Most of the parents are the worried lot. One does not know why things are leading to divorce. It looks; we have been observing so many of misunderstandings with the new couples. In some cases, in spite of counseling, people are not adhering and going in for divorce cases. It looks, there is somewhere, some problem exists.

In another known divorce case, one B Tech boy, software engineer married to one MCA girl. Within three months, the girl opted for divorce from the boy. One does not know any reason for this. The bride's parents looks to have played a major role in this. This incident happened one year ago. Both bride and bridegroom are presently living separately. The bride is yet to file a divorce case in the court of law. It takes another 3-4 years easily for getting divorce in the court of law.

Before the Marriage engagement function, Both the Bridegroom and the Bride have to register their names with the competent authority of that jurisdiction or with Sub-

Registrar of Marriages or any Authorized Nodal Agency or with any Government nominated Nodal Agencies either directly or through eSeva or Mee Seva Center's, and a Certificate to the effect that so and so would like to get Marriage engagement on such a particular day, month and year and following by Marriage on a particular day, month and year. This is only an intimation to the Government through proper channels, so that, the Government would be kept informed about the Marriage engagement and Marriage Function of particular Bridegroom and Bride. So also, local Station House Officer [Police Station] also to be kept informed about the Marriage engagement and Marriage Function with dates fixed for these functions. This will definitely, avoid future problems, troubles and other unforeseen marriage litigations and post-marriage complications, if any, arising out of misunderstandings in both the family groups. This system will work out well, and could possibly avoid post-marriage mis-understandings which may lead to divorce.

Presently, after Marriage is over, the new couple are going in for Marriage Certificates and approaching the Sub-Registrar's Office or any authorized e-Seva or Mee Seva Centre's for issue of Marriage Certificate.

These are all called post-de-facto Certificates.

In advance, obtaining the Marriage Engagement Certificate and followed by Marriage Certificate, could reduce divorce cases.

Parent's involvement with the young couples looks to be the primary aspect. Parents influence is the cause for many broken marriages. One does not know why parents to interfere in the newlywed couple's life. Always new couples should be asked to live separately.

Brides' parents in India are afraid to perform marriage to bridegrooms working at foreign countries, fearing break-in marriage may take place. Moreover, there are many marriage sites existing in the websites. It has become a very common feature to search for brides and bridegrooms. All personal profiles look to be good and attractive.

Now-a-days, every bride needs a software engineer bridegroom. The main criteria are the salary package of the bridegroom. How much bridegroom is earning. Whether the bridegroom is having any property, lands, own building or flat including a car. This is the criteria for any bride. Moreover, brides are not getting married up to the age of 30-35 years. These brides want to earn as much as possible before marriage takes place. This is the state of affair. When compared to present trend of marriages, alliances in olden day's marriage, alliances took place in a very simple manner. Though in olden days, there was no much of money circulation, all the marriages were performed well and almost all the marriages got well established. The problem has cropped-up, when the IT field is in full swing. It looks, IT field only the root cause for divorce cases and break-in-marriages. One will pray The God that no more divorce cases are foreseen in the near future.

The Vision of a Bride before marriage alliance is needed, so as to assess the bridegroom's habits. This vision is to be counselled to all would be brides well before hand. This vision will enable would be brides to assess the bridegroom's habits. If this is assessed well before hand, then there will not be much of Divorce cases in the near future. This type of vision is essentially needed in these years.

To some extent remedies, after marriage, to avoid divorce would also work-out. But, however, such remedies go a long way and sometimes it may work out positively or may not work. But divorce cases shall be avoided if proper care and remedies are taken. The first and the foremost point is to see that the Husband should not take any alcoholic drugs or drinks. This is the main reason where marriage life gets broke. For example, I will give below a small article like story, which will enlighten the couples and also would be bride and bridegrooms.

The main reason for the divorce is the habits of husbands. Husband's bad habits like drinking, drug addicting, gambling committing more debts and making uneasy environment in the family circles lead to Divorce. The remedies are essentially needed for such people. More of counselling is needed to such alcohol addicted husbands.

As an Author, I have number of friends who are regular drinkers in the social circles. Drinking alcohol is not an issue. One can drink on few occasions. There is no problem. But, continuously taking alcohol, day-in and day-out and dreaming high and building castles in the air, is not at all correct. Many people lost even their lives due to high and regular drinking. In this aspect, I would like to project few of the incidents below for the information and knowledge of all the readers.

DRUNKARDS live in third world, enjoy and dream more. In this world of life, some people are accustomed and habituated to social drinking of alcohol including wine, vodka, brandy, and cocktails. Taking alcohol in business sector for maintaining business relations is one thing. Consuming alcohol of different types including foreign brands, standard brands, local made alcohol by upper middle-class people are another thing. Enjoying all types of alcohol brands each day by middle class people and lower middle-class people on some occasions, looks to be common everywhere. Taking local made liquor and other local made cheap liquor and toddy is very common and frequent by the hard labor.

All the Governments are getting quite a good amount of revenue through the sale of different types of various liquor brands. Few Governments depend for substantial revenue through various types of taxes. Some Governments encourage liquor sales and some Governments do not encourage liquor sales. Few Governments, on earlier occasions banned liquor sales in their respective States, landed in trouble due to huge loss of Government revenue thereby failed to run the governance and administration and even lost the political power. On later years, the same Governments which banned the liquor revoked the sale of liquor to raise the revenue substantially.

Drinking alcohol in top circles (social, business, and political circles) has become the order of the day. Lest, it is difficult to maintain the good business-socio-political relations at all levels. Taking top alcohol brands, foreign brands, whisky and scotch in such top circles, looks to be a fashion and necessary; whereas, consuming liquor each day-in and day-out and partying every day may lead to problems. Few people only can afford to lead such lavish style of life.

Some upper middle-class people in various business fields and sectors take regular drunks. Mostly now-a-days is seen in Information Technology field, consume liquor on week-ends and enjoy a lot. But this is also a costly affair. Many people are in the middle-class sector habituated to liquor of all brands and consume liquor on daily basis, by spending their hard-earned money. Even hard labor consumes local made liquor brands each day by almost spending their 60 percent of earnings.

There are many risks involved after consuming liquor. Number of people each day fall prey to road accidents, while some people who drive in intoxicated condition their two and four wheelers also meet with accidents.

I have seen many people and few known friends who take alcohol on regular basis right from morning and evening are financially helpless condition to meet their family expenses and are unable to meet their regular needs for their children's education. It is quite a saddening affair. Even some people who consume liquor daily are branded as 'Drunkard' and no social respect is given to them.

I will give one example which I had. On one occasion, I engaged an auto-rickshaw to go to city shopping mall. The auto driver had put on start the digital auto meter. After passing some distance, I was getting some alcoholic type smell in the auto-rickshaw. I thought, it was some petrol or diesel smell. After some time, I thought it was gas auto-rickshaw. After few minutes, I thought it fit to ask the auto driver about the smell which was emanating from the auto. I was able to judge that it was alcohol smell coming from the auto driver. No doubt, I was correct in my thinking. It was alcohol smell. Then I asked the auto-rickshaw driver whether he was intoxicated with alcoholic drunk. He replied boldly, stating that Sir, I took a small quantum of liquor. I told him to stop the auto-rickshaw. Immediately, the driver of the auto stopped. I asked him, why you took alcohol when you are taking the passengers, while charging for auto service. Is it not your duty to see the passenger's safety? He politely replied, sir, sorry. It was a mistake taking alcohol and driving the auto. I told him that, if you continue to take liquor or alcohol at this middle age, then, I don't think you will live long and you will not be able to see your children's marriages and your grandchildren. Moreover, I told your spouse will have to do servant-maid job, or beg people for survival in case of any harm is done to your life.

I told the auto driver straight-away that, people who are intoxicated with third brand liquor, or local made liquor will not live long.

Then the auto driver replied, sir, I will stop drinking habit from now-on. The driver realized the truth in my speaking to him on the facts. I got down at my place and the auto driver refused to take auto charges for my good advice.

Drunkard habits are like this:

They abscond to offices. They never work. They make money by pledging various articles including gold and silver for the sake of drinking. They quarrel when they are in bad moods. They don't speak properly. They even speak vulgar language outside as well as at home. They even quarrel with counterparts and their own children. They live in third world and their dreams are high. They make unnecessary chit-chat, speak on waste subjects and make time pass without any productive work.

Intoxicated and drug addicted people never listen to others. They spend money towards alcohol, wine and on intoxicated items and never give money to their spouse and children.

I have seen many of the drunkards lost their jobs, dislocated their family status, landed in many criminal cases.

Generally, drunkards become gamblers in one way or the other. Gambling in the sense, playing cards, horse racing, Number games, Lottery, betting on various sports. It is observed that quite a number of horse racing punters consume liquor and bet during horse races on horses. It is very common that people play cards while consuming liquor of their choice and simultaneously smoke cigarettes.

One could see in many places very lengthy parked motor cycles and cards in front of wine shops, Bars and Restaurants, Toddy shops and in front of Janata Bars and Star Hotels. Many of the Wine Shops are located in thick residential places, near to temples, and even adjacent to schools/colleges/offices/bus stands/railway stations. Every drunkard spends money on local brand liquor and waste time, energy and loose health. Even some regular drunkard's beg small amounts of money and ask hot drinks from some known drunkard-mates.

Some Governments owned Wine Shops earn substantial revenue directly. All the people are influenced to take the liquor on one occasion or the other.

It is a very well-known fact, that in any major political election, municipal elections, local body elections, panchayat elections, company/factory elections, society elections etc., the liquor flows like water. Without the supply of liquor, people look like not tempted to work or participate in elections. These are the back-door methods to tempt a person.

Some people consume liquor due to frustrations, family problems, financial problems, domestic problems and what not problems. Of course, reasons are plenty to consume liquor. Persons who are alcoholics have one reason or the other to substantiate them. Naturally regular alcoholics will not find their growth easy. Their family life gets dislocated and disturbed. They often lose patience. They land in financial troubles. They never get social respect in family and friend's circle. They are never able to meet good medical treatments in needs of time, due to lack of funds. People never come forward to help morally or financially to drunkards.

In some States, liquor flow looks to be seen as more than cash flow. In some States and villages drinking water is not available to common person; but, all types of liquor is made available at cost. At some places, whoever purchases liquor, water of 100 Milli Liter or 200 Milli Liter sachets are given free of cost.

It is, many a times observed that drunkards and regular alcohol drinkers are always irregular to their professional works, due to uneasy, ill-health and hangovers. Regular drunkards mind will be very simple, that they want to consume liquor some-how. Drunkards always speak non-stop and good orators at that particular intoxication ti8me and power of speech will be more. They get extra energy at some particular point of time. But drunkards become weak and slowly lose their health and land in major health problems. Drunkard's longevity is reduced. Drunkards lose their social status, family reputation will be lost, living standards will fall-down, and social respect will be lost, children's education will be disturbed and many long run family troubles and disturbances are to be foreseen, which even can lead to divorce of husband and wife, all due to consumption of alcohol, infighting within the family and domestic circles will be frequent and regular.

For alcoholics and drunkards, there are de-addiction centers, rehabilitation centers, nature cure centers and many other Non-Governmental Organization centers could be seen at number of places. Such centers addresses could be located through search engine websites like yahoo.com, google.com, rediffmail.com etc.

Drunkards can reduce their drinking habits, smoking habits and other narcotic drugs habits slowly, if they want to stop consumption of all types of intoxicated items. Every person has got The God given Will Power. All the good habits Pay on one day or the other to a person and for bad habits one has to pay the cost at one time or the other.

Literary Field on WORDS and WORDS

Words meaning never be the same The usage of words meaning will be different.

NON-LINGUISTIC LANGUAGE is generally mingled and used in other languages by many people, when they are at other languages spoken places.

Even the foreigner's languages are quite often mingled with other languages due to expression of words and speaking problem People who live in State/Country borders, the impact of mingled or clubbed languages used will be high and is very often observed.

European languages like Italian, Russian, Spanish, Greek, Latin, are sometimes inter and intra-mingled and like that in Indian Languages, Sanskrit, Pali, Devangari, Dravida, Arabic, Parsi words are mostly mingled and inter & intra-connected while speaking and writing. In the present globalization scenario, many words of different country's languages are used very often so that people are able to understand what the other person is saying.

People like motherland and mother tongue language, respect their language and shower affection on their local language and would like to express their feeling while speaking/writing. This is called Sahityam, which speaks of literary expertise in respective living literary areas.

The language spoken/written indicates people's culture and national integration.

The word makes magic in our lives. The love, passion fashion, mission, relation etc will be in order, when we use words properly, sensibly and tactfully.

Languages are made to use accordingly to the situation using proper proverbs, quotations, phrases, short stories, examples, experiences to give effective suggestions when people in problems will definitely give solace when you work with proper modulation.

It gives more impact and importance to the situation.

When you want to give the information, you should use words properly and with firm voice.

Use minimum words and try to convey the message.

Lengthy and deviated conversation weakens the purpose.

They may lose the interest to get information or suggestions.

All the time we cannot practice the type of procedure.

By seeing the situation, we can change phrases, quotations, proverbs make the conversation very interesting and effective.

A balanced positive talk with durable pleasant positive vibration makes the other person feel like spending more time in your company.

A kind of bond will be created.

We should use the language with proper pitch and it should depict your feelings, emotions, reactions and your moods.

Accordingly, the other person should understand and react into the situation.
The language or the words should convey the message correctly without confusion.

Practicing this usage of words is very easy.
Keep the mind cool and clear in your thoughts.
Be firm when you want to convey the message.
Do not get confused when others disturb you.
While you talk with others, words usage should be limited.

When you put it on the paper it can convey the message properly and completely with balanced good expression.

Indian languages have so many appropriate, expressive words.

We can play with the words to convey any impression, expression, emotion, reaction or feeling and son on.

But think with the mind, heart and soul.
Think in a positive way and deliver with proper words.
People should remember and think of you like a human being.

Another important aspect which could change and transform your life in a better way by increasing your influence and improving your relationship and lead to the road of success depends on using the words carefully while speaking to others.

The words are very important and powerful tools and it all depends on how you use these words.

As explained in earlier lectures, these words carry tremendous energy of your strong intent or will.

The energy of confidence, the energy of your assertiveness and these words which are nothing but sounds carry a very powerful magnetic field which is very intelligent.

When these words are spoken with 100 percent pure intent, honesty, conviction etc of the positive energies, it will affect the magnetic field of listener or listeners.

Every human being, being a magnetic will have his own magnetic field which is invisible and forms a circle around the body.

When we give speech in the form of words of magnetic sounds, it touches the magnetic field of listeners and in physics one reaction takes place which is called as inductance.

Here, when they are meeting at one point, there will be an exchange of energies and these energies carry your thoughts, your suggestions, your ideas your concepts.

If your thoughts are full of inner conviction, honesty, pure in nature, will definitely influence the magnetic fields of listener in a very positive way and all will be attracted towards how you and will be more receptive.

While addressing, you should also follow certain tactical steps which we have already described in various prerequisites like change your voice i.e., modulating your voice ups & downs will also have a very good positive impact on others.

This was proved by the scientists working at NASA.
Vedas are recited with a very specific and particular modulation of voice.

When you speak this way, sending the messages in the form of mantras create a very magnetic field which will influence the magnetic fields offers and brings about a positive reaction and response.

Hence, try to culture your voice and you can practice at home, learn how to modulate the voice, when to take the voice up, when to take the voice down.

But one thing, use words in a very proper way.
They should be very polite and very appealing.

I also give lot of importance to the usage of words and nothing but words, because the words are the only powerful tools of the communication.

If the words are not there, there is no communication and when there is no communication there is evolution.

Hence, try to use words very sparingly and talk only when you required.
Thus, you can conserve lot of inner energy.
One small wrongly used word will spoil the entire interview or inter-personal relationship.
Hence, always practice and practice your presentation at home.

One very well-known marketing or a director of a very big pharmaceutical company who had graduated from the Business School of Harvard University had the habit of always doing the presentation all alone much before the actual meeting begins.

I had seen lot of seniors and highly successful people plan much before and list out things on a piece of paper, make rehearsals, before the actual presentation and achieved tremendous success.

Only one word about which most of the people, mostly the ‘teenagers do not understand, but use vey frequently the word as “individuality”.

Without knowing the deeper meaning of this word, it is misused, misunderstood and misinterpreted by most of the people.

A teenage boy or a girl when the elders comment about their dressing code, they react that they had their own individuality, they had their own freedom to wear what they would like to wear.

This they call as individuality.

According to them individuality means to have their own freedom starting from the dressing code, their physical appearance, their conscious, their ideas, they germ all these in one single capsule called individuality.

But, one thing they forget is all these impressions, ideas; concepts are formed by watching around their environments.

The type of movies now-a-days they see, the type of magazines, the type of advertisements, the type of concepts they are highly influenced by the surrounding environment.

Even the greatest scientists they confirm those factors with more than genetic effect, the environmental effect works on the personality of the human beings.

Unfortunately, the reading hobby has come down and the type of books available in the market they will never help in the self-development of the individual persons.

The idea, the concept or the personality trades of the writers are imposed on the young readers who could not differentiate between what was required for their personality development, but on the contrary their emotions are easily influenced.

As discussed in earlier lectures, the human beings could be stimulated or through their emotions rather than their intellect or the rational thinking.

The same thing here, it is applied by the producers, directors, actresses and the politicians, the entire environment does not give practical meaning for life.

They always take you in higher up in the fantasies in the dream world.
They always take you away from the reality.

That is the reason most of the teenagers are frustrated and before they realize their potentials, most of them are becoming addicted to alcohol.

Most of celebrities are having depression, frustration, anxiety, and neurosis and are terminating their lives.

The reason is very simple. It is nothing but the influence of the external factor is influencing your inner personality.

Right from the child-hood, your college atmosphere, the school atmosphere, the ragging by the senior students, in the most uncivilized ways and then the pictures you see, the books reading, the magazines you are reading and the type of friends and the type of movies, all these are making the artificial personality.

Earlier, the scientists used to behave with the genetic influence would be more on the personality trade, but the recent studies have proved that the environment influence is greater than the genetic influence.

Now-a-days, the entire generation is under the influence of the surrounding environment.

Thus, the real potentials are masked by the artificial real personality trades.

There is always a conflict between the natural personality trades and the acquired personality trades from the surrounding environments and the social conditions.

That is the reason the teenagers are unable to resolve the inner conflicts, one is natural and the other one is unnatural.

This is the reason most of the youngsters are terminating their lives before realizing the potentials.

The influencing personalities like the cinema stars both actresses and actors are super imposing on the natural personality trades of the youngsters mostly the teenagers.

That is how they lost their own hidden potentials and talents.

Mostly, they have become imitators than originators.

They are capable of producing and contributing so many useful things to the entire world, but unfortunately as informed earlier, that their own personality is being suppressed as they imitate the personality trades of the actors and actresses.

The quality of the movies, of late, has come down with lower and lower moralities.

Actually, there are no moralities at all in the movies.

The visual impact is always more influencing and that is what happening at this time and even the advertisements are misleading.

The celebrities do not care for the welfare of the society and for the sake of money, even promote the cheapest products.

The common people will imitate the same thing like smoking cigarettes or using sub-standard products since their beloved heroes advertise.

Thus, unfortunately, the present youth is embracing the un-useful personality trades of the people whose contribution to the society is less than zero.

At least, time has come for the present youth. This is a wake-up call. Don't be an imitator. You have tremendous potential.

Try to imitate patriots, the greatest people who have contributed to the society and to the common people of this world.

Also, try to logically analyse what is the meaning of individuality.
You cannot have your own freedom when you are living in a society.

For example, you are studying in a particular school and the school decides the uniform which could be standard for all the students and if you rebel and refuse to wear because there your individuality was hurt, then you will be losing the opportunity of studying in the school along with other students.

Similarly, if you refuse to follow the dress code in an organization, then you will not get a job.

The present youth of India have got great potentials to develop their own personality instead of being an imposter.

Spend time qualitatively.
The life is a gift from the God and use the life for the betterment of the society.

Expand your consciousness and live life independently with your own inborn personality trades.

Now, we are dealing with some of the negative energies.
I don't wish to call them as prerequisites.

Now-a-days, the entire world is suffering from one disorder or disease called depression or frustration.

These two are negative energies, but, in my view and frustration are very common.

There is nothing negativity in these energies.

Even the most successful people when they were interviewed confessed that they have also passed different phases in life, the negative energies like depression, anxiety, and frustration.

Most of them could come out from these energies within short span of time.
When a human being is sick immediately the doctor will advise some pathological test.

The patient will be weak, he will have high temperature, he will not have appetite and the blood report reveals there was a presence of bacteria and increased number of WB cells which forms the defensive mechanism of the human body.

Similarly, depression is also a mental action to an inflection.
This is very common and natural.

Every human being, at one stage or the other will have to pass through these depressions, frustrations, anxiety and lot of other negative energies.

But only thing is that this depression we should not analize it to survive for a long time.

So, what is the best way to combat this depression or anxiety?
Even in my case, I had depressions and frustrations on many occasions.
But I allow it to exist for not more than 15 minutes.

What I do is that, I immediately change my clothing, I take fresh bath, sing a song and whistle the song, and I think all positive achievements in the life and I just go out for a walk, maybe I go to restaurant, have snacks, tea and relax myself.

The depression has gone within 15 minutes.

Whenever you undergo depression or a frustration, just think of the best moment you had in your life and think all your best achievements in your life.

Every human being is born with tremendous potential and is capable of doing many greater things.

Unfortunately, because of environmental influence one gets depression.

But he starts remembering his positive achievements and how he had achieved set goals in his life and how he was successful in different fields, he goes to the past and thinks about the happiest moments, the energy of depression will be dissolved and disintegrated immediately.

When you start thinking off your own achievements slowly you gain confidence and when you gain confidence the depression cannot survive in the company of confidence.

I am once again repeatedly assuring and emphasizing that every human being including the most successful people in the world have passed this depression, anxiety, frustration and disappointments and negative energies.

But the great quality they had is all are optimistic and hopeful for their future and constantly put forth their efforts.

Similarly, even a common man can become a celebrity or could become potential contributor for the good cause of the society.

For God's sake, do not to be worried or scared about depression, frustration and they are the part of the life.

Sometimes, the depression will stimulate self confidence in most of the people who have positive thinking.

This is also a feedback mechanism.

If Mahatma Gandhi was not insulted and not thrown out of the compartment and abused, he would have not become a great leader.

Similarly, you can see the life history of great people, all negative situations, and negative events made them very strong.

Then why you can't? You can also become and achieve greater things in your life. Never give up hopes always live with hopes.

After the storm, there is always calm. After the sunshine there are showers of rain.

I once again appeal to all the youngsters, kindly think that you are also made by the God, and the God's creation there are no clause.

Similarly, in you there is no clause, you are born to do greater things.
You are born to achieve so many things.
You are born to contribute to the society many good things.

Do not give up.
Wait and wait, try and try, you will definitely achieve your respective goals.
There are so many books which are written on Human Management.
But these books are not necessary to be appropriate in all the situations.

The human beings are different throughout the world because of their cultures, their habits, and their customs.

What is applicable in India may not be applicable in other foreign countries like African continent or in European countries.

These books will only help to a certain extent. What you need is your own analysis, or own logical deductions.

Whenever there are failures take some time, analyse and immediately take remedial measures.

Constantly you have to do self-analysis that is the best way managing the human beings rather than reading the books and applying the same.

The only exceptions in some of the books, which discuss the basic psychological trades, are very useful.

The Upanishads are the best human management books because they have discussed the human personality trades in depth.

As a Training Manager, I read only few books on human management and was not convinced except some books which deal with the human psychology.

I have given lot of examples from my own experience under this title The Game of Life. Basically, if you want to be successful you have to take lot of interest in other human beings.

By reading books, you are not able to achieve anything.

By reading the human beings in your own practical way, you would understand them and then when you apply the set principles definitely you will be more successful.

The same law is not applicable to every case of human beings.

You need to change your strategies in the same interview many times.

When the customer is closing the door your approach, you need to open another door. When closes that door, try to open another door.

In between these spaces, you should be able to assess the personality of the other human being and then open the door very wide.

I have tested all these in my personal.
Hence my humble request that you read more and more about human beings' personality and have your own experience.

Your own experience is the best teacher and the best guide to you.
It does not mean that you should not read other books, but you can read other books.

I try my best to list out all the important prerequisites, but there are many more that you need to find out for yourself.

It is also equally difficult thing for me to write-down lot of other training methods or techniques which could consume volumes and volumes and it would not be appropriate to put those things in our website.

However, those who are interested they van contact me on my contact phone.
Life is an interesting game.
Take lot of interest involving you.
Play the game according to the rules & regulations and improve the skills and enjoy yourself.

==========

Dr. APJ Abdul Kalam's Brief Life History

Date of Birth, Mother & Father, Native Place:

Avul Pakir Jainulabdeen Abdul Kalam was

Born on 15 October 1931 (83 years old)

Date of Death: 27 July 2015

Born to a Tamil Muslim family in the pilgrimage centre of Rameswaram.

83-year-old Kalam, who collapsed while delivering a lecture at IIM, Shillong, and died,

Dr. APJ Albdul kalaam's Father Jainulabdeen was a boat owner.

Imam of a local mosque;

His mother Ashiamma was a housewife.

Dr. APJ Albdul kalaam's studied at Madras Institute of Technology, and completed his

Degree in Aeronautical Engineering in 1960.

Defence Research and Development Organisation (DRDO)—an Indian Military Research Institute— at Hyderabad.

Later the Indian Space Research Organisation (ISRO).

Official Works:

DRDO acquired approximately 2100 acre of land in 1970's for the purpose of Anti-Tank Missile Testing.

Dr A.P.J. Abdul Kalam the then Director of DRDL persuaded Govt of Andhra Pradesh to give the land for setting up RESEARCH CENTRE IMARAT (RCI)

The area occupied by RCI *has been named as Vignyana Kancha.*

On 5th Aug 1985, former Prime Minister Late Shri Rajiv Gandhi laid the foundation stone for this establishment.

Former President of India Shri R. Venkatraman inaugurated the laboratory on 27th Aug 1988. RCI, a premier R&D organization in the country with an objective of developing frontier technologies for Defence applications.

RCI has considered as 'Avionics Hub' of DRDO. It is one of the three DRDO Labs of 'Missile Complex'.

He is called as "Missile Man of India"

For his breakthrough development of

"Ballistic Missiles and Launch Vehicle Technology"
A.P.J. Abdul Kalam, Indian scientist who was President of India from 2002 to 2007.

APJ Abdul Kalam Technological University (initially Kerala Technological University), a State Government University has come into existence on May 21, 2014.

The Dr. A. P. J. Abdul Kalam University is located at lush green area on the new Indore (Madhya Pradesh).

Invention Pokran Trails

Invention - Kalam - Raju Stent

Invention - Lightweight Calipers

Invention - Project Devil and Project Valiant:

DR. APJ ABDUL KALAM'S QUOTES.

WINNERS ARE NOT THOSE WHO NEVER FAIL BUT THOSE WHO NEVER QUIT.

ACCEPT YOUR PAST WITHOUT REGRET, HANDLE YOUR PRESENT WITH CONFIDENCE AND FACE YOUR FUTURE WITHOUT FEAR.

LEARNING GIES CREATIVITY,

CREATIVITY LEADS TO THINKING,

THINKING PROVIDES KNOWLEDGE,

KNOWLEDGE MAKES, YOU GREAT.

A DREAM IS NOT THAT WHICH YOU SEE WHILE SLEEPING

IT IS SOMETHING THAT DOES NOT LET YOU SLEEP.

THE BEST BRAINS OF THE NATION MAY BE FOUND ON THE LAST BENCHES OF THE CLASSROOM.

IF YOU FAIL NEVER GIVE UP BECAUSE "FAIL" MEANS "FIRST ATTEMPT IN LEARNING"

YOU CANNOT CHANGE YOUR FUTURE.

BUT, YOU CAN CHANGE YOUR HABITS. AND SURELY YOUR HABITS WILL CHANGE YOUR FUTURE.

"WHEN OUR SIGNATURE CHANGES TO AUTOGRAPH, THIS MARKS THE SUCCESS".

TO SUCCESS IN YOUR MISSION, YOU MUST HAVE SINGLE-MINDED DEVOTION TO YOUR GOAL.

DREAM, DREAM, DREAM

DREAMS TRANSFORM INTO THOUGHTS

AND THOUGHTS RESULT IN ACTION.

(THERE ARE THOUSANDS OF QUOTES OF DR. APJ ABDUL KALAM).

DR. APJ ABDUL KALAM WAS VERY FOND OF TEACHING SMALL KIDS, STUDENTS, AND TO IIM OR IIT STUDENTS.

The Story of Farmers Satisfaction

There was a village in a remote area. In that village there was a farmer. The farmer has 100 acres of farming and cultivable agricultural land. A river also flowing in adjacent to the famer's agricultural land. This farmer has Two Songs, of course, well qualified and educated. Instead of doing a job in the city, these two sons preferred to work in their own land. They had a plan of action. To make these 100 acres of land most useful for all the villagers. So, the father farmer and two sons decided to sell off 25 acres of land and build a beautiful mini city. Even they have taken care of to avoid damages from Tsunami. To avoid from burglars, these two sons had adopted one poodle. To safeguard their wealth. The father, and two sons maintained good health by doing yoga every day. These two sons never drink any vodka. Even these two sons never took Tea or Coffee. These two sons had good fruits and banana regularly. They had very good professional skills. These two sons had a check-list and pert-chart and were very principled in their daily life. Firstly, these two sons built a bungalow by investing some amount which they received, out of sale proceeds of their 25 acres of land. The father performed elder son marriage. The bride and the daughter-in-law felt happy to have a good husband. These two sons boycotted their crocked friends. Even these two sons enjoyed travel in the ship and cruise, as a holiday trip. These two sons, of course, knew well swimming. Even these two sons had a mountain hill trekking, as a hobby and adventure. These two sons never touched any meat including beef.

The father and two sons, ultimately built a mini-city in their rest of 75 acres land. Also, this mini-city has cinema hall, mini-hospital, paid hostels, some shops, a medium school etc by having a master plan. These two sons had also taken necessary government persons.

The dedication and commitment they had made this mini-village possible. Ultimately, the dream of father and two sons fulfilled.

All the local people and nearby villagers enjoyed the fruits in later years.

The theme is, a good timely thought and a good planning makes a person successful and feels gets highest satisfaction in the life.

THE HYDERABAD (TELANGANA STATE, INDIA) IS A GOOD PLACE TO LIVE IN

Every country needs professionally qualified and high intellectuals to all the global States especially in India in particular. These professionals, intellectuals, economists, technologists, analysts, business tycoons, socialists and philanthropists so on and so forth, are to be given motivation, encouragement, support and to take care of by the Government. The services of these persons are essentially needed for the all-round development in the fields of science & technology, defense, agriculture, culture, information technology, games & sports, entertainment, product development, manufacturing, financial services, education, pharmacy, and more particularly in technology development & research development activities.

It is a setback to India, if high profile and very important people's services are not utilized properly for the growth, development and upliftment of poor people. Moreover, India Government always works for the bene3fits of pro9-poor people and for improvement in living standards & for economic growth.

It is up to the Central Government and respective State Governments, how best the services of these high-profile Civil Services professional services are utilized for the purpose of running the State Administration with good governance, especially in major financial matters. The sound financial position improves the ability of Government's function to work for all round development of State in particular and the Union Government in general.

The entire Telangana State is a peaceful State. One can do business, study and live happily without confronting any troubles. Moreover, the State Government's good governance is also a plus point. Policing is very good. Law & Order is good. Traffic Management is good. Roads are good. Drainage system is being improved with latest technology. Un-interrupted power supply is foreseen. All the Public Sector, Private Sector, Banks, Industries, autonomous bodies, schools, colleges, universities and other business establishments including Trade & Business, Petty business people are happy in their fields without confronting any type of dislocations or disturbances. Government is running its own Telangana State Road Transportation Corporation (TSRTC) busses to all the nook and corners of the Telangana State of Ten Districts.

India Government is trying to have Foreign Direct Investment (FDI) program, for setting up manufacturing & production units in India. This also coincide Make in India Program of the Government of India. If investors come forward from global countries under this FDI program, India will benefit in all round development in the science & technology and in other fields. Also, there will be many employment opportunities for all sections of youth and people. If things, as expected by the Government, become in reality then India will become "second manufacturing factory" in the globe, as the 'China is the first manufacturing factory' to supply various items to global countries.

Really, the Telangana State is a good State for people to live in and lead their life happily. The seasonal rains come in time. No water scarcity. The Hyderabad city is one of the best cities in the country as per various survey reports. It is a best place to live in. Moreover, all the districts in the entire

Telangana State, would, in the next span of five years, become "role model districts" in India, and one will expect lot of development almost in all the fields, while competing with world class developed States in maintaining international standards.

BUSINESS STRATEGY

A SPECIAL NOTE ON COMMERCIAL ASPECTS AND PROJECTS CONSTRUCTION ACTIVITIES (in India) AND REAL ESTATE FORMATION OF NEW TWO STATES AND TWO GOVERNMENTS INVESTMENT, TRADE AND BUSINESS

-

In view of the formation of Two New Telugu Speaking States (TELANGANA STATE (wef 2nd June 2014) – presently consists of 31 Districts) and ANDHRA PRADESH STATE (wef 8th June 2014) – presently consisting of 31Districts). It is very obvious that these are good Governments and does good Governance. There is good stability in these two new States is foreseen. There is all-round development is foreseen in all the fields including establishments of Charitable Institutions/NGOs/TRUSTS/FOUNDATION CENTERS, CONSTRUCTION, REAL ESTATE, FLATS, MALLS, INTERNATIONAL SCHOOLS, BUSINESS MANAGEMENT COLLEGES, HOTEL INDUSTRY, FUNCTION HALL BUILDING CONSTRUCTION, TOURISM SECTOR, CHARITABLE INSTITUTIONS/NGOs/TRUSTS/FOUNDATI

ON CENTERS INCLUDING SOCIAL SERVICE ORGANIZATIONS, ITIR Sector HUB (Information Technology and Investment Sector) AND EDUCATION HUB.

These Two Governments are stubborn, strong and capable of doing effective good Governance for the next 5-10 years' time. It is worth investment for new Projects and new establishment's set-up, at this juncture, because there is lot of encouragement from these new Governments. In my opinion and observation, there will not be any major -agitations -troubles -dislocation of business and industrial sector -economic disorders, no riots, no communal harmony, no major strikes. Lot of development and growth is foreseen in the near future.

-

Till before bifurcation of Andhra Pradesh into Two States (presently Andhra Pradesh with 13 Districts and Telangana with 10 Districts including Hyderabad), Hyderabad has been the IT Hub, Pharmaceutical Hub, Real Estate Hub, Education Hub, Industry & Manufacture Hub, Public Sector and Private Sector Hub, Trade and Business Hub, Tourist Centre Hub , Agriculture Hub, Movie Industry Hub, likely to be the Aerospace Manufacturing Unit Hub and more than all, Hyderabad & surrounding areas are the Hub for petty businesses and Cosmopolitan City with people staying with different culture, regions, language from various States in India including foreign people studying at Hyderabad.

Also, many Public Sector Enterprises, Private Sector Industries, including various types of Manufacturing units right from Small Scale Sector, Medium Scale Sector and Large-Scale Sector are available for the manufacture of various items, viz, electronic goods, pharmaceutical items/medicines, agricultural products, garment industry, Construction material industry and other small, medium and major products of all types. The Telangana State is having Man-Power Resources, Pharmacy raw-material Resources; Agricultural Seeds Resources, Software Development Resources, Research & Development Activities, Science & Technology, Sports & Culture, Fisheries development, Tourism Activities, Film Industry, Wine manufacturing Industry, Hotel Industry (Restaurants, Bars, Resorts, Lodging facilities 2/3/4/5 Star), Steel Industry, Printing Technology Industry, Paper manufacturing Industry, Herbal manufacture Industry, Plastic Industry, Leather Industry, TV-Press-Media-Print Industry, Transport Industry (Tourist Busses, Two/Four Wheelers, Material Carriage & Transport vehicles), Grain Industry, Food Industry, Wood-Mattress & Furniture Industry, Glass & Crockery Industry, Cosmetic & Perfumes Industry, Number of Small Scale

Industries, Light and Heavy Industries, Cable Wire manufacturing Industry, Pre-fabricated Building Material Industry, Chemical Industry and many more Industries and Activities including Social Service Oriented Charitable Institutions/NGOs/Trusts and what not.

Since the combined Andhra Pradesh officially bifurcated into two different States, lot of encouragement and motivation is seen in all the above fields. Most of the people likely to settle down at Andhra Pradesh in view of the growth, development and new set up & establishment of new Andhra Pradesh State, the Telangana State including Hyderabad with 10 Districts is presently and likely the hot place for above fields/sectors. Moreover, the weather conditions suit to most of the above fields particularly to the IT, Pharmaceutical, Agriculture, Foreigners for Investments, and Trade & Establishments. Moreover, the Hyderabad city (Telangana State) is situated above 560 feet approximately of seal level. Apart from this, there are no communal riots, strikes, disturbances, tsunamis, earth-quakes, political disturbances and the Hyderabad city is quiet and calm for all category people for staying purpose, education, trade, business and also for major investments. Also, since the new Telangana State 5-Year Term Elections recently completed (May 2014) and the new Government has taken over for Governance of the Telangana State Administration and likely and expected to last for complete 5-year Term 'without any major disturbances and without political uncertainty'. Therefore, it is quite evident from these facts that now the Investment, Trade and Business in all the above-mentioned fields/areas are sure to establish and flourish at Hyderabad city and in its surrounding areas. Presently, lot of hectic activity is foreseen in all the above activities/fields.

INVESTMENT, TRADE AND BUSINESS will improve and also the Government is encouraging Investors, to come up with their Business Plans, Trade Plans and Investment Plans. Also, INFORMATION TECHNOLOGY INVESTMENT REGION (ITIR) is likely to be set up and get established in the near future at Hyderabad where lot of improvement, development including employment opportunities would be provided to IT and Non-IT qualified persons/people. As it is, Hyderabad is called the IT Hub where quite a number of IT establishments already exist especially at Hitech City, and at Uppal area of Hyderabad. As it is IT Hub at Hyderabad is one of the biggest in India when compared to other States and already proven successful for investments and business deals worldwide and well recognized by the global countries. Therefore, it is needless to mention that this IT Sector and the ensuing ITIR sector will definitely make the Hyderabad City in particular and the Telangana State in general to compete with the global standards and competitions and put the Hyderabad City in the Driver's seat, as far as IT field is concerned, in the near future. Also, Hyderabad city area and its surroundings are most suitable for IT field and also for Tourism Sector because of its environmental weather conditions, climatic conditions and also for Accommodation facilities are available for all the people working. These climatic conditions are most suitable for foreigners when they visit Hyderabad for various official visits and also for staying purposes.

As regards other fields, Hyderabad city (Telangana State) is well ahead of other States in the fields of Education, Real Estate, Electronic Industry, Technology Development, Science & Technology, Construction field, Tourism sector, Film Industry, Pharmacy, Hotel Industry, Agriculture, Horticulture, Research & Development and in Social Service Activities (Charitable Institutions/Trusts/NGOs/Foundation Centres), so on and so forth and made all round progress, development, well recognized by the global countries and well applauded by the Centre.

There is really a Real Estate Boom, in both these Two States. There is likely hectic Construction activity in both these Two States, is in offing and foreseen up to next 5-10 years' time. Lot of development is expected to be seen with regard to Trade, Business, Market, Industry, Agriculture, Science & Technology, Film Industry, Software Industry Educational Industry, Hotel Industry and other fields of development Domestic, National and International interest areas.

But, however, presently, one can expect profit returns moderately up to 5 years period. But definitely, the investment is safe due to increase in land values. As regards, NGOs/Trusts/Foundation Centres, Charitable Institutions, Trade & Business, Colleges/Schools, Flats construction, shopping complexes construction and doing business, the profit would be foreseen only after five years, from the Trade and Business Operational and Commencement time.

I shall be able to provide the required Project Report(s); relevant to various above stated areas, without financial aspects (financial aspects will be given at appropriate time when really going in to start the Project).

-

Moreover, Charitable Institutions/Establishments/Trusts/NGOs are also existing at Hyderabad and surrounding areas. The Charitable Institutions with the following activities are working for the cause and benefit of the Less Privileged children/people. Lot of demand and new likely Charitable Institutions establishments are likely to be set up in the near future.

CHARITABLE ACTIVITIES

- MOTHERLESS BABIES ORPHANAGE HOME
- HOME FOR AGED
- HOME FOR WIDOWS
- HOME FOR WIDOWERS
- BABY CARE HOME
- HOME FOR DISTITUTE STREET CHILDREN
- HOME FOR SENIOR CITIZENS
- MUSICAL INSTRUMENTS
- HOME FOR YOGA, MEDICATION AND ASANA
- NATUROPATHY HOME
- DE-ADDICTION HOME
- PHYSICALLY HANDICAPPED CHILDREN EQUIPMENT HOME
- FUNCTION HALL
- HOME FOR DISPLACED WOMEN
- ABACUS LEARNING HOME FOR

CHILDREN
- OBESITY REDUCING CENTRE
- GYM EXERCISES CENTRE
- SLIMMING EXERCISES CENTRE
- SWIMMING POOL (OUTDOOR)
- MEDITATION CENTRE
- PRAYING ROOM

As such, this is the time for any Investor to come forward for Investment purposes at Hyderabad, in its surroundings and also in all the 10 Districts of new Telangana State. It looks that the Investments are safe and Return on Investment (ROI) are very much foreseen, as per the Investment Pattern and Investment Plans. If one goes by the previous Track Record, no business person or investor who invested amounts for various types of businesses as above stated went Red nor put into loss.

Good Construction activity is likely expected on all fronts, such as, Flats, Malls, Offices, Multiplexes, Schools/College Buildings, Hospitals, Movie Houses, Shops, Fly-over Bridges, Software Offices and all-round development, in these Two New States, because of Trouble-free areas, Peaceful States, suitable Weather and Climatic conditions especially for Information Technology Field set up, establishment, and improvement. Likely coming soon Information Technology

Investment Region (ITIR) in both these newly formed States, in the Southern Region of India. Also, there is lot of demand for National and International Schools/Colleges. All-round Construction and Development is foreseen within the next 5-10 years' time.

Lot of Real Estate & Construction of Buildings demand is foreseen, in the near future. It is, in my opinion, advisable to go in for Real Estate and Investment side, Procurement of Land, go in for construction activity and to set up the Institutions/Organizations/Offices/Colleges/Malls/Flats/Multiplexes/Industry/Hotel Industry and Tourism Industry etc.

I shall be able to provide the required Project Report; relevant to various above stated areas, without financial aspects (financial aspects will be given at appropriate time when really going in to start the Project). The Financial Budget supposed to be invested by the Investor would depend on the proposed Business Plan and the Business proposal.

Please note that there are number of procedures/systems, Government formalities and documentation, Permissions, Approvals, Licenses, Certifications both Trade and Quality, fee, taxes, Municipal Permissions, Construction Plan Approvals, State Sales Tax, Central Sales

Tax, Value Added Tax (VAT) Submission of Income Tax Returns under IT Act, Banker's requirements, Local Body requirements etc. are to be followed, in every type of Project commencement and during the operational period.

=========

My Life and My Story

MY LIFE FROM CHILDHOOD DAYS

Way back in 1955, I never knew myself
I was at my small Railway Quarters
Then studying 2nd standard
A small place called Boiguda
A central place to Secunderabad Railway Station

Famously called twin cities,
Called Hyderabad and Secunderabad

Thin population,
Nowhere seen cars,
Few Double Decker buses,
Plying with Dakota buses
Only Government jeeps and few bicycles
No Auto Rickshaws
Very little single buses,
No scooters seen, only one or two
No cars seen, only countable cars
Only Tangas that is Jhatkas
Very few cycle rickshaws
Very few Government schools
People never knew outside world
No radios, no transistors
Countable cinema theatres
Ignorant of worldly affairs

The life was sleeping life
No wine shops, no bar shops
Only Pan shops here and there
Cigarette sales in good numbers
Pan chewing people in good numbers
Foreign cigarettes plenty

Life those days, just a get going one
No gas stoves, only coal fire for cooking
Famous days for Powder Milk
Commodities not costly
Available at very cheap costs
Available commodities plenty at small cost
Every item available
No pollution, no cheating
No deceiving, no faction fighting

Those days were memorable ones
Those days were enjoyable ones
Those days were trouble-free days
Those days understood days
No telephones
Only telegrams
Post cards, postal covers
Communications very slow
Small roads, one or two, street lights
No water connectivity no bore wells
Pleasant days with no fast development
Can't go here and there
Only walking system
No good education

No private colleges
Government colleges' countable ones
Plenty Government jobs

Qualified people very limited
No money, no cash flow
No real estate, no construction
Slow process, slow development
Public Sector factories
Slow recruitment
Banking Sector jobs
Slow recruitment
Government jobs
Slow recruitment
People started settling at twin cities
Families joining twin cities
Population started increasing
Shops started setting up
New start-ups and new private offices
Days were slowly rolling
Developments are in slow pace

Radios came in
Transistors came in
Autos with motor mechanism came in
Old buses replaced with new ones
Bicycles seen on roads plenty
Lambretta scooters seen plying plenty
New cars on roads seen plying
Plying jeeps for government offices observed

More movie theatres constructed
Business seen improving
Cash flow looks to be improved
New technologies came in
People started educate, became qualified
Things moving at fast pace
Construction of independent houses seen
People started settling
Cash flow vastly improved
People became polished
Political scenario changed
People became political awareness
Groupism commenced
New political parties floated
Many drastic changes took place
The scenario of twin cities changed
Developments took place
Expansions took place
Roads widened
Municipalities came in
Corporations established
Houses and office buildings constructed
Population increased
Private colleges set up
Government offices expanded
Banking system enlarged
Cost of living index increased
Factories set-up
Private offices set up
Political awareness increased

Business set-ups grown
Universities increased
Change in education system came in
New Technologies invented

THE NEXT DOOR BEAUTY

This is real, I was at twenties
Just young as anybody else
Fast, brisk, sportive, active
I was in full swing with full of strength
I was doing physical exercises then

I completed job oriented courses
Like Typewriting and Shorthand
Searching for government jobs vigorously
I was deeply thinking in the balcony
This was everyday thinking in the morning
I was neatly dressed, ready to read newspapers
I had a sip of coffee too
I was myself busy in my own works

The days were such, a job was essential
No other go, except to hunt for a job
Days were rolling, thoughts were running
Finding out then source identification
To follow, government procedural systems
Jobs were plenty but process was slow
Just managing those days without a penny
My everyday balcony affair, reading
newspapers

Status co, no development for few months
The next door, a beautiful young girl was watching me

I could not observe her many days
I was involved in my own thinking

The girl was able to understand my agony
I was at my balcony, she was at her balcony
One day, I saw her and noticed that she was looking at me

I casually wished her with my hand
The girl reciprocated wishing me back

My concentration diversified on various aspects
I packed my job issues then
I was very regular, in time at my balcony
The beautiful girl also maintaining my own timings

I looked at her, but, secretly looking at her
I wished to speak to her, but I was afraid
I wished to see her straight, but I was not daring enough

I wished to meet her, but my legs were not moving

I wished to write a letter, but my hands were not moving

I wanted to express her something, but my brain became stand still

I was to move away from my place
But, my body became stiff
Day moved like a week
The Week moved like a month
The Month moved like a year

My mind was upset
My movement became halt
I was not moving here and there
Traffic signal, not got green signal

My body became heavy
My body temperature reaching sky high
My thinking was running fast

My ideas were generating fast, but not reaching the girl

I was jeopardized
I was left alone
I could not express anything to anybody
I became helpless and nervous

It looked the girl opposite next door liked me
I was thinking in positive aspect
I was imagining that the girl liked me
But, there was no progress in communication

My expressions were not reaching the beauty girl

My ideas were not reaching the glamorous girl
My hopes of talking to the girl, got failed
The girl looked to be taking the things easy
Days and months prolonged
I could not catch up the sequence
I joined in a government job
I was immersed in my profession

The next door beauty girl was a beauty girl
I missed a chance to tie a knot to the beauty girl
I remembered the girl long years
I was helpless, due to my pre-occupation

So, never miss a beauty girl
Try and try at last one will succeed
Timing is important to tie a knot
Opportunity comes only once
Never miss the opportunities
Best of luck to all those guys in love like matters

TODAY'S YOUTH – TOMORROW'S LEADERS

Today's youth of the nation are all tech-savvy
Broad-minded and rebellious with vast ideas

Could mobilize people of all religion
Caste and creed as the youth of India play
Crucial role in promoting communal harmony

Will lead to socio-economic constitutional changes

Maintaining peace in the country
The youth are the future leaders of tomorrow.
The youth's education in
Engineering
Medical
B Pharmacy
Bio-technology
Automobile engineering
Research & Development
Management and
In all fields of study
Can mobilize people due to professional understanding

In maintaining peace and communal harmony

No interfering in issues like caste, creed, religion or ethnicity.

Tech-savvy youth spreads the peace, love and communal harmony

Good social media tools like Face book, Linkedin, Twitter, WhatsApp

Blogs. Rapid changes took place
Fine Arts play an important role

In spreading the message of brotherhood and peace

Young authors, writers, poets and artists come together

Enlighten people of India about the secularism in Indian Constitution.

Can understand the culture at major cities like Mumbai and Delhi.
The youth cares for personal growth based on their talents.

Youth having good jobs by virtue of their talent
Can bring changes on people around them
Maintain peace and harmony in the society
The government has to work with the youth

Bring about unity in diversity for the future of nation.

YOUNG AUDIENCE GRAB & CONQUOR SOCIAL MEDIA

The younger audience use social media
Youth use social media technologies too much

INDIA, Land of Opportunities:
The younger generation and audience,
Look for quickest communication
Quick Return on Investment (ROI) and money

The days are rolling-out with updated new technologies

The fields are-
Research & Development
Pharmacy
Agriculture
Software Development,
Science & Technology
Sports & Culture
Tourism and Film Industry
Liquor Industry
Steel Industry
Printing Technology
Plastic Industry
Leather Industry
TV-Press-Media-Print
Grain Industry,
Food Industry
Wood-Mattress & Furniture Industry
Glass & Crockery Industry
Cosmetic & Perfumes Industry,
Pre-fabricated Building Material Industry

Now I am 75 running.

My memories Flash Back
I am confined to house
My Four Grand Children are pretty
I look after them and monitor their movements
I act as Security to my Family and Children
I play with my Grand Children
I enjoy my Life by playing with my own people

I too visit all my relations house for various functions

I am happy that I am on Earth by the Grace of God.

I hope to complete my Century.
I maintain good habits and good principled diet.
I never take any outside food.

I am happy, active, brisk, and reasonably knowledgeable.

I Pray the Almighty to give me good health, if not any wealth.

I am satisfied with what I have.
…….

I am very happy that
I am with my children, my grandchildren,

My kith and Kin, My Friends and Relatives

I am enjoying this World
This Glittering World is good
I think this World is a Heaven's Branch
All Apsaras do come, visit this World
This is an Angels World, Never before I saw
A Great World with Beauties
I have an ambition
I am making a small research
My Memories are recorded in a small Chip

I would like to carry this Memory Chip along with me

When I Die.

Looking out all the possibilities for a Special Chip

Yas, it looks to be possible through R&D
Fulfilling the ambitions Yas or No
The God only knew well.
As a Human Being, I am to be optimistic

Hope to be successful for a Memory Chip to carry to Heaven.
But, may not be possible before I complete 100 years.

I hope for the best for future generations.

....

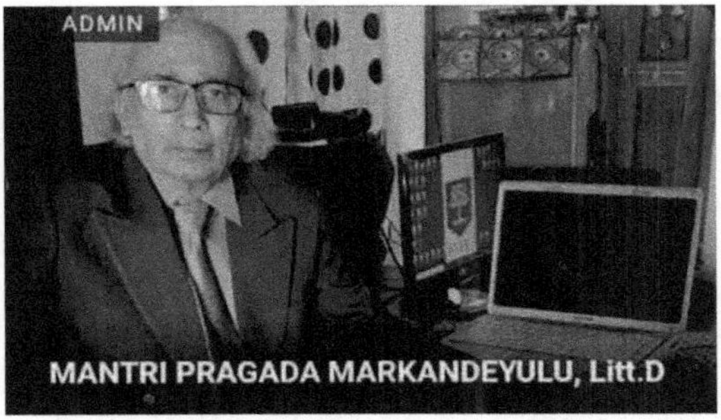

MANTRI PRAGADA MARKANDEYULU, Litt.D.,
Poet, Novelist, Song and Story Writer
B. Com, DBM, PGDCA, DCP,
(Visited Nairobi-Kenya, East Africa)
(Retd. Public Sector Enterprise Officer)

- The State of Birland (Bir Tawil) Representative at Hyderabad-India (www.birlandgov.org)
- **CESAR VALLEJO AWARD 2021, UHE, Peru for Literary Excellence**
  - The Silver Shield Award from UHE, Peru for my Literary Excellence 2021.
  - 2021 GOLDEN EAGLE WORLD AWARD FOR LITERARY EXCELLENCE, HISPAN WORLD WRITERS' UNION Peru
  - Gujarat Sahitya Academy and Motivational Strips LITERARY EXCELLENCE Honor
  - *Honored with "Royal Kutai Mulawarman Peace International Institute, Philippines"*

- *Royal Success International Book of Records 2019 Honor, Hyderabad-India*
- *Institute of Scholars Research Excellence Award-2020, Bangalore (India)*
- *Gujarat Sahitya Academy and Motivational Strips 2020 Honor, Gujarat-India*
- *Hon. Doctorate in Literature from ITMUT, Brazil. (2019)*
- *Literary Brigadier Honor (2018) from Story Mirror, Mumbai, India*
- *Spotlight Superstar Honor (2018) from Story Mirror, Mumbai, India*
- *Golden Ambassador General for Development and Peace at World Peoples Forum @ TWPF/BTYA, Bangladesh*
- *State of Birland at Bir Tawil Recognized Poet*
- *RKMPII Nobility Award 2021*
- *RKMPII HEART OF GOLD NOBLES Honor Certificate 2021*
- *ISFFDGUN Internationally Accredited Certificate 2021.*

Hyderabad - Telangana State (INDIA)
Email: mrkndyl@gmail.com
+91-9951038802
+91-8186945103
Twitter: @mrkndyl68

CPSIA information can be obtained
at www.ICGtesting.com
Printed in the USA
LVHW100347011222
734242LV00009B/177

9 789356 754157